# Baby Dolphin

## AT HOME IN THE OCEAN

WRITTEN BY SARAH TOAST
ILLUSTRATED BY GARY TORRISI

Publications International, Ltd.

In the warm waters near the shore, a herd of bottlenose dolphins plays among the waves. Two leap together high into the air, then they arc and dive in. Two others ride the surf on an incoming wave.

The dolphins move their tail fins up and down to gain speed. They use their flippers to make sharp turns and quick stops.

A small group of dolphins hunting for fish comes up and "blows" together. The dolphin in the front is Mother Dolphin. She must go to the surface to breathe through her blowhole.

Dolphins find fish by making clicking sounds and listening to the echoes that bounce back. The dolphins talk to each other by whistling and calling.

Mother Dolphin and two other adult dolphins find a school of small fish in the shallow water of a bay. The dolphins rush at the fish.

The fish are swept up in the wave and pushed ahead of the speeding dolphins. They land on the sandy shore. The three dolphins snap up the fish and slide back into the water.

Soon Mother Dolphin will be ready to give birth. She has help from two dolphin "aunties," who stay next to her. Other dolphins from the herd gather around them and whistle softly.

As soon as Baby Dolphin is born, the two helpers guide her to the surface of the water for her first breath. After she breathes, Baby Dolphin can float.

Mother Dolphin nurses her hungry Baby Dolphin near the surface of the calm ocean water. Mother Dolphin floats on her side and squirts her extra-rich milk into her baby's waiting mouth.

Baby Dolphin floats near the surface so she can breathe while she is fed. The "aunties" stay nearby and encourage the mother and baby with soft sounds.

Mother Dolphin stays beside her baby throughout the summer. The "aunties" also take care of Baby Dolphin.

Baby Dolphin is very playful and curious. She can swim well and loves to nudge her mother.

Baby Dolphin is growing fast. Soon she will grow a thick layer of blubber to help her float and keep warm.

Baby Dolphin is quick to learn each dolphin's whistle. The dolphins in the herd also bark, click, moan, and mew to keep in touch with one another and express their feelings.

The dolphins work together to take care of Baby Dolphin and the other young dolphins. They cooperate in feeding and defending the herd.

The dolphins are all spread out when a shark swims close to their group.  Grown-up dolphins quickly surround Baby Dolphin and all the other young ones to protect them.

Four other grown dolphins rush toward the menacing shark. The adult dolphins ram it hard with their beaks, lifting it clear out of the water.

The shark flees, but some of the dolphins are exhausted and hurt. They help lift each other to the surface so they can breathe through their blowholes.

The danger is gone, but Baby Dolphin stays close to the older dolphins. Baby Dolphin floats up with Mother Dolphin to take a breath of fresh air and rest for a short time.

After the dolphins have rested, they celebrate by playing games in the warm water. Baby Dolphin flips through the air and uses her tail to splash her friends.